MEDICAL BREAKTHROUGHS

THE DISCOVERY OF GERMS

A GRAPHIC HISTORY

BRANDON TERRELL

ILLUSTRATED BY JOSEP RURAL

GRAPHIC UNIVERSE™ • MINNEAPOL

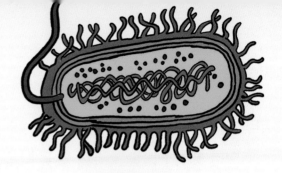

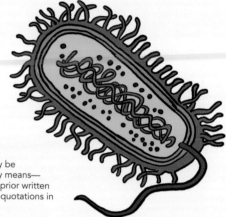

Brandon M. Terrell (1978–2021) was a talented storyteller, authoring more than one hundred books for children. He was a passionate reader, Star Wars enthusiast, amazing father, and devoted husband. This book is dedicated in his memory—happy reading!

Graphic Universe™
An imprint of Lerner Publishing Group, Inc.
241 First Avenue North
Minneapolis, MN 55401 USA

For reading levels and more information, look up this title at www.lernerbooks.com.

Main body text is set in Dave Gibbons Lower. Typeface provided by Comicraft.

Library of Congress Cataloging-in-Publication Data

Names: Terrell, Brandon, 1978-2021 author. | Rural, Josep, illustrator.
Title: The discovery of germs : a graphic history / Brandon Terrell ; illustrations by Josep Rural.
Description: Minneapolis : Graphic Universe, [2022] | Series: Medical breakthroughs | Includes bibliographical references and index. | Audience: Ages 8–12 | Audience: Grades 4–6 | Summary: "Earth is home to trillions of germs. But for most of human history, people didn't know they existed! Learn how the microscope changed everything, allowing scientists to see germs—and discover their surprising benefits"— Provided by publisher.
Identifiers: LCCN 2021014433 (print) | LCCN 2021014434 (ebook) | ISBN 9781541581524 (library binding) | ISBN 9781728448695 (paperback) | ISBN 9781728444123 (ebook)
Subjects: LCSH: Microbiology—Juvenile literature. | Bacteria—Juvenile literature.
Classification: LCC QR57 .T464 2022 (print) | LCC QR57 (ebook) | DDC 579—dc23

LC record available at https://lccn.loc.gov/2021014433
LC ebook record available at https://lccn.loc.gov/2021014434

Manufactured in the United States of America
1 – CG – 12/15/21

TABLE OF CONTENTS

CHAPTER 1:
WHAT ARE GERMS?

Our galaxy is a vast and wondrous place.

The Milky Way contains Earth and its solar system. This galaxy is home to at least 100 billion stars.

But that number is tiny compared to the number of germs on Earth.

Scientists estimate there are trillions of germs living on our planet. That's more than a galaxy's worth of stars!

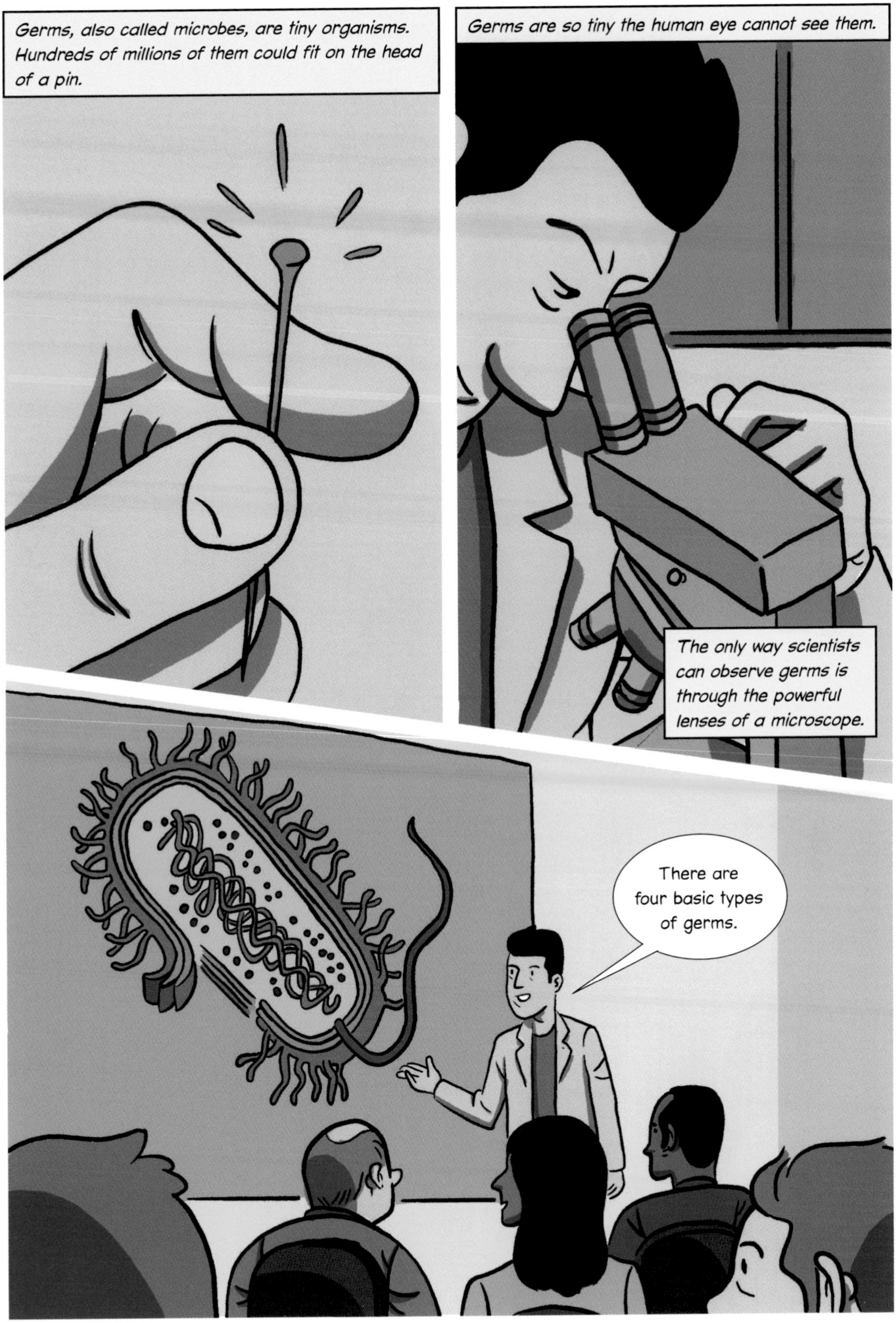
Germs, also called microbes, are tiny organisms. Hundreds of millions of them could fit on the head of a pin.
Germs are so tiny the human eye cannot see them.
The only way scientists can observe germs is through the powerful lenses of a microscope.
There are four basic types of germs.

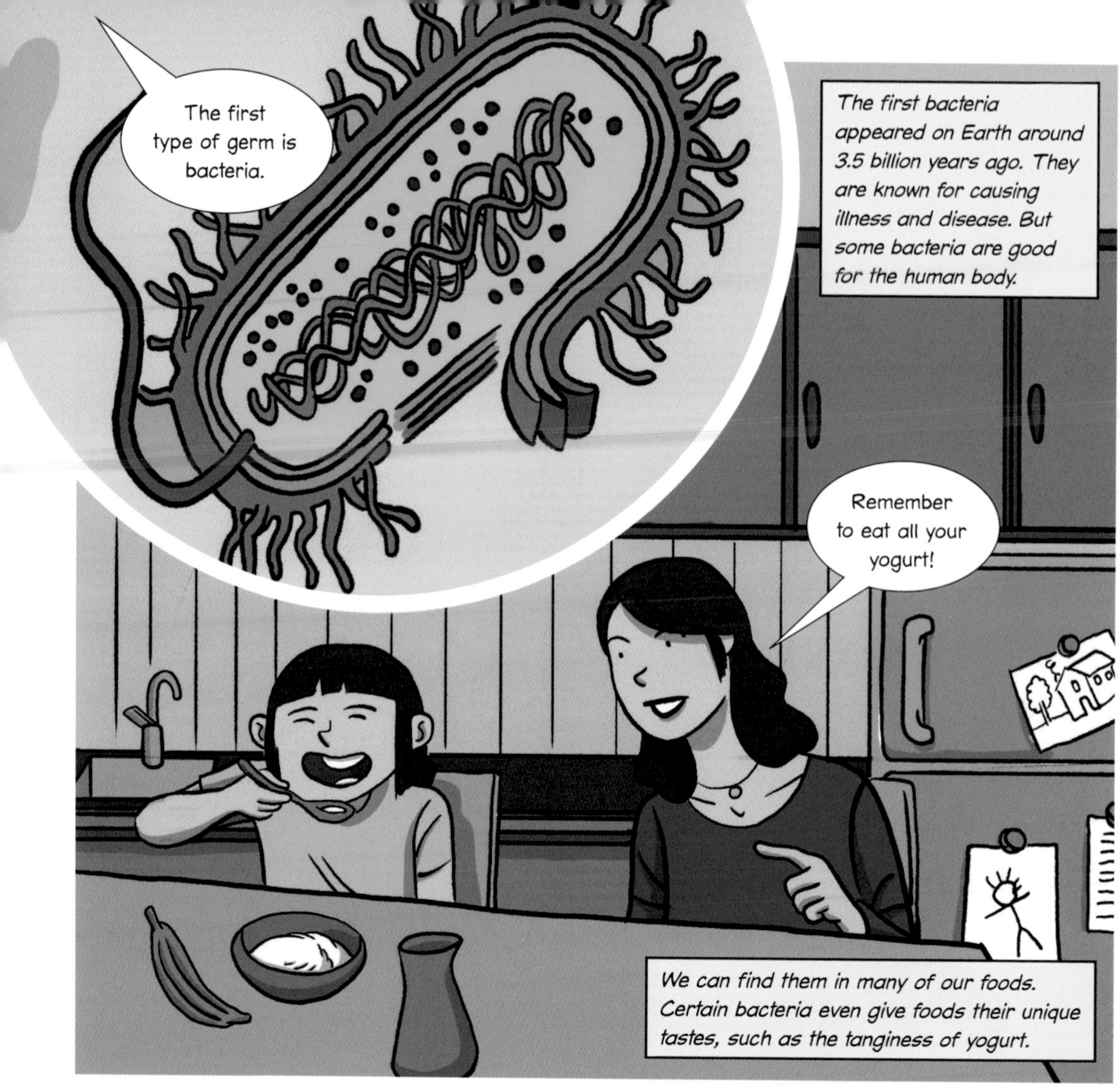
The first type of germ is bacteria.
The first bacteria appeared on Earth around 3.5 billion years ago. They are known for causing illness and disease. But some bacteria are good for the human body.
Remember to eat all your yogurt!
We can find them in many of our foods. Certain bacteria even give foods their unique tastes, such as the tanginess of yogurt.

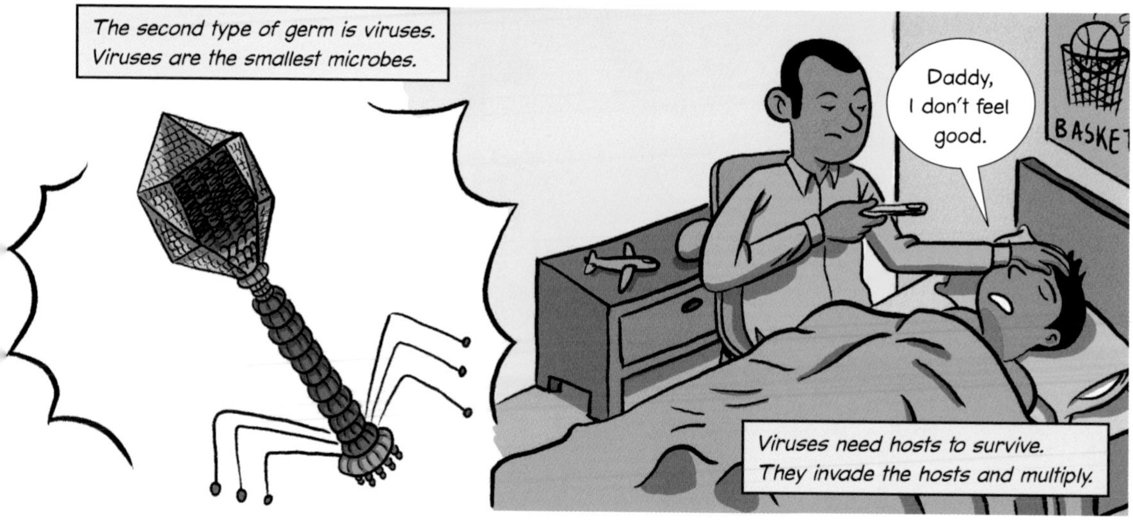
The second type of germ is viruses. Viruses are the smallest microbes.
Daddy, I don't feel good.
BASKET
Viruses need hosts to survive. They invade the hosts and multiply.

The third type of germ is fungi. Fungi range in size from microscopic to very large. They are found on land, in water, and in or on plants and animals.

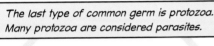

People can eat some fungi, such as mushrooms. And scientists can use others, such as mold, to create medicines.

The last type of common germ is protozoa. Many protozoa are considered parasites.

Protozoa need water to live. They thrive in lakes, rivers, stagnant ponds, and damp soil.

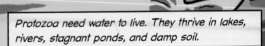

Modern scientists know a lot about germs.

Take nice, easy breaths. Don't worry, we'll have you feeling better in no time.

But how does the human body protect itself against germs? And how did doctors fight germs before they even knew they existed?

CHAPTER 2

THE BODY'S NATURAL DEFENSE SYSTEM

Unseen microbes are all around us. The human body uses its immune system to recognize and kill the harmful ones.

The immune system is like a castle that defends your body against invaders.

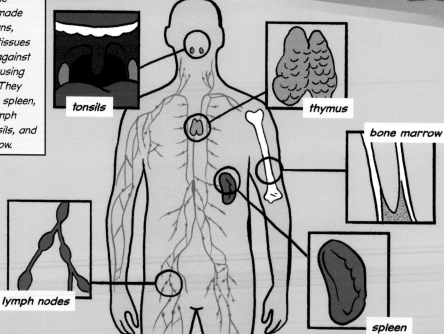

The immune system is made up of organs, cells, and tissues that fight against disease-causing microbes. They include the spleen, thymus, lymph nodes, tonsils, and bone marrow.

tonsils

thymus

bone marrow

lymph nodes

spleen

The human body also has ways to stop germs from entering in the first place.

The epidermis, or skin, acts like a shield. Skin keeps germs out while letting in water and nutrients.

The human nose creates mucus to trap germs and small particles as we breathe in.

And eyelashes prevent small, sometimes germ-carrying particles from entering the body through the eyes.

Enzymes in our tears also kill germs.

Harmful germs cause a variety of illnesses in humans. However, for many centuries, scientists didn't even know germs existed!

So, people all over the world developed different theories about where sickness came from and how to cure it.

Doctors in many early cultures, including ancient Egypt . . .

Greece . . .

. . . and the Roman Empire believed that too much blood caused sicknesses. They used a technique called bloodletting to drain blood from the patient's body.

Hundreds of years later, in fourteenth-century Europe, a bacterial infection called the Black Death killed tens of millions of people.

Plague doctors treated patients while wearing masks stuffed with sweet-smelling herbs and dried flowers. They hoped the masks would protect them from the disease.

At the time, many thought the disease was carried by vapors or bad smells. Doctors later learned the deadly plague mostly spread by fleas carried by rats. The bacteria entered the human body through flea bites.

It wasn't until doctors and scientists were able to see microscopic germs that they could study and understand their effects.

CHAPTER 3:
LOOKING CLOSER

In the early 1590s, Zacharias Janssen of the Netherlands changed the way people saw the world.

I've done it!

Janssen was the son of an eyeglass maker. He used his knowledge of lenses and optics to create a new device.

Janssen's creation was known as a compound microscope.

This is fabulous, son! What a creation!

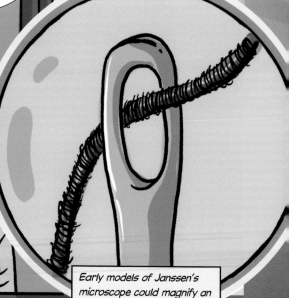

It used two lenses. The first, known as the eyepiece, was where the user placed their eye. The other, the objective lens, pointed toward the object.

Early models of Janssen's microscope could magnify an object up to nine times larger.

The Janssens weren't the only ones working on a new magnifying instrument. Fellow Dutch eyeglass maker Hans Lippershey was developing a compound microscope at the same time. This caused some confusion over who the real inventor was.

But Lippershey would later patent another amazing invention: the telescope!

Janssen's invention was revolutionary. But at first, people mostly considered the instrument a novelty.

Ha! Yes! I can see the flea in great detail!

Father, let me look! Let me look!

It took another seventy years before the microscope became a common scientific tool.

In 1609, famed Italian astronomer Galileo Galilei improved on Janssen's design. He began using lenses with shorter focal lengths.

Galilei later called the invention the occhiolino or "little eye."

In the 1660s, British scientist Robert Hooke helped design an updated microscope.

He used it to examine the structures of snowflakes, plants, and insects.

Hooke documented his findings in the 1665 book Micrographia. The illustrations of magnified objects and animals in Micrographia caused a stir.

They may be detailed, but I can't believe these drawings are real!

Then, in the late 1660s, Dutch cloth merchant Antonie van Leeuwenhoek further improved microscope lens design.

Hmmm. Yes, I can see the tear.

Van Leeuwenhoek was an ordinary working person. But he had many interests and talents.

I find this device fascinating. Did you know Robert Hooke used something similar for *Micrographia*?

Van Leeuwenhoek developed a simple, one-lens microscope that was more powerful than any before it.

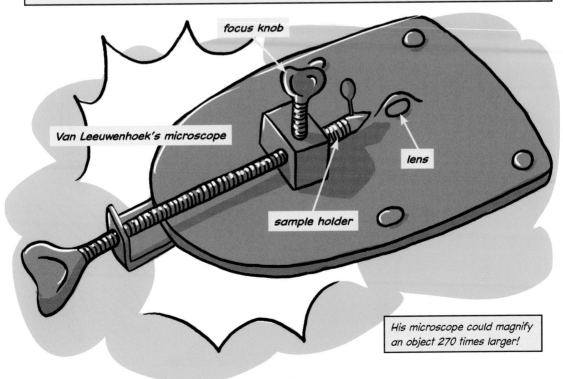

focus knob

Van Leeuwenhoek's microscope

lens

sample holder

His microscope could magnify an object 270 times larger!

Van Leeuwenhoek began to examine different things with his new invention.

One day, he scraped some of the plaque from his teeth.

What he found under the microscope would make history.

There's something moving on the plaque!

Van Leeuwenhoek had discovered bacteria!

In September 1683, van Leeuwenhoek wrote a letter to the United Kingdom's scientific Royal Society to share his findings. He described seeing tiny living creatures through his microscope. He called the creatures "animalcules."

The biggest sort . . . had a very strong and swift motion . . . like a pike does through the water. The second sort . . . oft-times spun round like a top . . . and these were far more in number.

At first, people did not believe van Leeuwenhoek's discovery.

Preposterous! It cannot be true.

Animalcules? Who has heard of such a word?

Did he really see all these things? Highly doubtful.

But scientists soon confirmed that his findings were true. Because of this discovery, van Leeuwenhoek would later be called the Father of Microbiology.

Even after van Leeuwenhoek's findings, it took many years for scientists to agree over what the tiny creatures were and where they came from. Many scientists believed they could grow from non-living materials such as dust and dead tissue. This belief was known as spontaneous generation.

They can't simply appear out of nothing!

But some scientists were not convinced of spontaneous generation.

In 1859, French chemist Louis Pasteur conducted an experiment that disproved spontaneous generation.

These germs didn't appear from nothing . . .

The experiment showed that microorganisms entered a flask from the air.

. . . they contaminated my experiment from elsewhere!

Pasteur's work also helped prove that germs caused disease after entering the human body. This idea is known as Germ Theory.

More research followed scientists' acceptance of Germ Theory. German physician and bacteriologist Robert Koch studied the connection between germs and disease.

Koch and his team also created new ways to study germs in the lab.

The blue stain colors the bacteria. Now we will see them against the background tissue!

In 1876, Koch found that bacteria caused the infection anthrax.

He developed a way of staining bacteria samples to see them better under the microscope. This was a huge step forward in germ study.

By the 1870s, Louis Pasteur was an expert in the study of germs. He began examining chicken cholera, a bacterial disease that affected breeding hens.

Pasteur and his team injected chickens with a small, weakened dose of the cholera bacteria.

The sample was left alone for a month. The bacteria must have weakened in this time.

They discovered that after exposure to the weakened bacteria, the chickens were more likely to fight and survive the disease at full strength! This was the first lab-produced vaccination.

In November 1921, Scottish doctor and bacteriologist Alexander Fleming made a very fortunate mistake.

While he was sick, a drop of mucus fell from his nose onto a bacteria sample.

Fleming wondered if the mucus might affect the growth of the bacteria.

What do you know? I was right. The bacteria have dissolved!

He discovered that lysozyme, an enzyme present in bodily fluid, killed germs. It was an important step in scientists' understanding of the human immune system.

Fleming's second accidental discovery happened in 1928 after returning from a family vacation.

Let me just take a quick look at those petri dishes I left out.

What in the world? There's mold on these slides!

Liquid produced by the mold had affected and killed the sample bacteria. Later, this finding led to the development of antibiotics.

CHAPTER 4:
CURES AND THE FUTURE

As treatment against germs progressed, so did the microscope.

In 1931, German scientist Ernst Ruska, along with his mentor Max Knoll, introduced the first electron microscope.

An electron is a tiny particle with a negative electric charge. An electron microscope fires a beam of electrons at an object to magnify it.

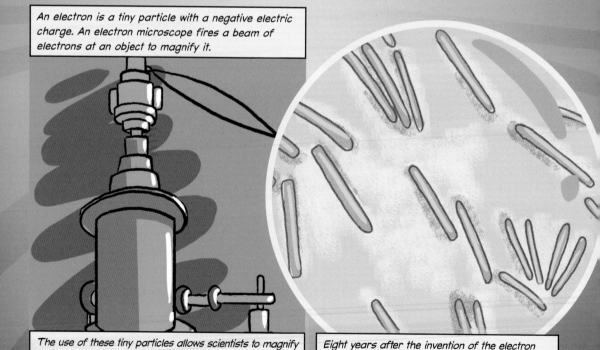

The use of these tiny particles allows scientists to magnify an object as much as 700 times more than a standard optical microscope. With this new technique, scientists could see the interior structures of plant and animal cells.

Eight years after the invention of the electron microscope, researchers used it to observe the tobacco mosaic virus. This marked the first time a virus was successfully viewed under a microscope.

In 1948, scientists used an electron microscope to identify the differences between the smallpox virus and the chicken pox virus.

In the decades that followed, electron microscopes also helped the discovery of many new viruses.

In 1989, for example, scientists were able to identify the Ebola infection of a monkey colony brought into Reston, Virginia, for research.

Electron microscopes have evolved greatly since Ruska and Knoll's initial creation.

In 2008, California's Lawrence Berkeley National Laboratory installed the TEAM 0.5 electron microscope. At the time of its creation, the TEAM 0.5 was the most powerful microscope in the world.

In addition to medical advancements, scientists are discovering other ways that microbes can be useful.

In 2009, scientists from the University of Edinburgh, Scotland, developed a harmless strain of E. coli bacteria. The bacteria produce a protein that senses trinitrotoluene (TNT), a chemical compound used in explosives.

This process causes the bacteria to emit light. When added to minefields, the ground lights up where explosive landmines are hidden.

In 2016, the US Geological Survey began a study into a strain of the bacterium Pseudomonas fluorescens. The study showed that these bacteria slow the growth of a plant called cheatgrass.

Cheatgrass is a straw-like weed that easily catches fire. Using bacteria to slow the plant's growth may lower the number of wildfires that occur each year.

Architects are also studying how to incorporate microbes into modern building designs.

In 2016, the Public Safety Answering Center II was built in New York City. The building design includes a wall of plants.

Microbes in the plants' roots filter out toxins. The plants generate oxygen too, creating a healthy working space.

Bacteria also generate an electrical current. Researchers at Lund University in Sweden are trying to capture this energy and transfer it to an electrical conductor.

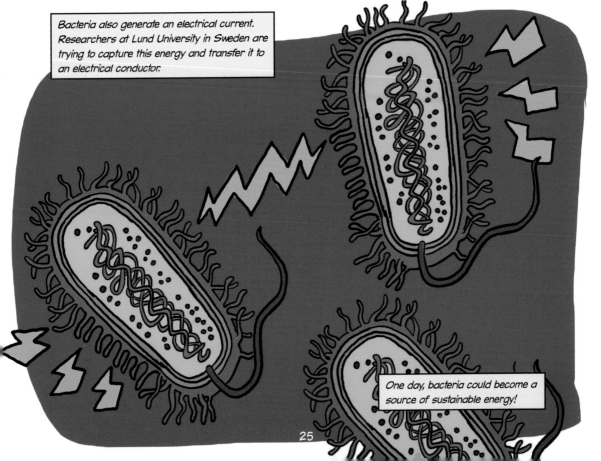

One day, bacteria could become a source of sustainable energy!

Seeing and understanding germs helped change the way doctors tackle disease. Modern medicine can prevent the spread of colds, the flu, and other sicknesses more easily.

And yes, your immune system is like a castle protecting you from invaders. But there are ways you can help it out.

Wash your hands often and thoroughly, using soap and water.

And when you can't wash your hands, use hand sanitizer.

Clean the surfaces of your home to keep them sanitized and disinfected.

And be sure to get plenty of rest each night.

Germs are all around us, but they aren't all bad.

Yahoo!

Dinner time!

Some germs help decompose dead organisms such as leaves. This process releases carbon dioxide gas, which plants use while turning sunlight into energy.

Others are in our food, making dough rise and cheese age.

Ha! Be careful there.

Although we often cannot see them, germs are an amazing part of our world.

SOURCE NOTES

17   George Dunea, "Van Leeuwenhoek's Discovery of 'Animalcules'," *Hektoen International*, Fall 2018, https://hekint.org/2018/10/23/van-leeuwenhoeks -discovery-of-animalcules/.

GLOSSARY

antibiotic: a substance used to kill or inhibit bacteria

enzyme: a complex protein produced by living cells that brings about or speeds up reactions

focal length: the distance from the surface of a lens to its point of focus

infection: the invasion of the body by harmful microorganisms

organism: a living thing that can function on its own

parasite: a living thing which lives in or on another living thing

plague: a disease that causes death and spreads quickly among a large group of people

plaque: a sticky film on teeth caused by bacteria

revolutionary: being or bringing about a big or important change

sanitize: to make sanitary (as by cleaning or sterilizing)

toxin: a substance produced by a living organism that is very poisonous to other organisms

vapor: fine particles of matter (like fog or smoke) floating in the air and clouding it

FURTHER INFORMATION

Alexander, Lori. *All in a Drop: How Antony van Leeuwenhoek Discovered an Invisible World*. Boston: Houghton Mifflin Harcourt, 2019.

Britannica Kids—Germ
https://kids.britannica.com/kids/article/germ/442739

Farndon, John. *Tiny Killers: When Bacteria and Viruses Attack*. Minneapolis: Lerner Publishing Group, 2017.

Kiddle—Germ Theory of Disease Facts for Kids
https://kids.kiddle.co/Germ_theory_of_disease

KidsHealth—What Are Germs?
https://kidshealth.org/en/kids/germs.html

Mould, Steve. *The Bacteria Book: The Big World of Really Tiny Microbes*. New York: DK/Penguin Random House, 2018.

INDEX